Discovering Churches

LOIS ROCK

A LION BOOK

Copyright © 1995 Lion Publishing
Illustrations © 1995 Lion Publishing

The author asserts the moral right
to be identified as the author of this work

Published by
Lion Publishing plc
Sandy Lane West, Oxford, England
ISBN 0 7459 2920 6

First edition 1995
10 9 8 7 6 5 4 3 2 1 0

A catalogue record for this book is available
from the British Library

Printed and bound in Singapore

Acknowledgments

The author and Lion Publishing wish to thank the following people for their help and advice:

Simon Danes, M.A. (Oxon.), Head of Religious Studies, Senior Master, The Bishop's Stortford High School

Philip Hewitt, R.E. Advisor, North Eastern Education and Library Board

Reverend Peter Hyson, Vicar, Aldbourne, Wiltshire

Reverend Phillip Tovey, Vicar, St. Francis L.E.P., Banbury Team Ministry

Delyth Wyn, Children's Work Organiser, Presbyterian Church of Wales

Sebastian, Daniel and Davina Rock for their contributions on pages 11 and 20.

Many thanks also go to the various churches who contributed pictures, artefacts and people to appear in this book, and especially to the Parish Church, Goring-on-Thames, for the loan of items on pages 5, 7, 11, 12, 13 and 17, and to the Parish Church, Eynsham.

British and Foreign Bible Society: for Bible extract on page 9. Scriptures quoted from the Good News Bible published by The Bible Societies/HarperCollins Publishers Ltd., UK © American Bible Society 1966, 1971, 1976, used with permission.

Photographs

A. C. Photographics: front cover (bottom left), 18 (bottom left)

Alexander, David: 14 (centre right)

Andes Press Agency: front cover (bottom right), 1 (main), 2 (top right), 3 (main), 6 (top left), 12 (top centre), 15 (main), 20 (top right)

The Bible Lands Society: 14 (bottom right) ©The Bible Lands Society, High Wycombe. Used with permission.

Catholic Herald: 3 (bottom right)

Ffotograff: title page, 2 (bottom right), 4 (centre left), 5 (centre left, centre right), 7 (centre right), 8 (centre left), 9 (top centre), 10 (bottom left), 12 (top right), 13 (centre), 17 (bottom left, centre left, centre right), 19 (centre left), 20 (bottom left, centre top)

Halliday, Sonia and Laura Lushington: 9 (centre bottom)

Jackson, Wendy: 5 (top centre left), 10 (top right)

Jones, Christopher: 8 (top right)

Lion Publishing: front cover (main picture), 2 (bottom left), 3 (top right), 16 (top left), 18 (top left), 19 (centre top, centre right), 20 (bottom right); John Williams: front cover (middle inset x 2), 1 (bottom centre), 5 (bottom left), 7 (bottom left, centre left, bottom right), 8 (bottom right), 9 (top right), 10 (centre right), 11 (bottom left, top right), 12 (far top right, bottom right), 13 (bottom right), 14 (centre left, centre top, centre bottom), 15 (all except main picture), 16 (centre, centre bottom, bottom right, top right), 17 (top right), 18 (bottom right), 19 (bottom left, centre bottom)

Press Association: 6 (centre left)

Rock, Lois: 1 (top left, centre left), 2 (centre left), 4 (bottom right), 5 (bottom centre, bottom right, top right), 7 (top left, top centre left, top centre right, centre left), 8 (top left), 9 (top left), 10 (centre), 11 (bottom right), 13 (top centre), 17 (bottom right), 18 (centre, centre right, top right), 20 (centre right)

Rous, Nicholas: 2 (centre right), 4 (top left, bottom left), 7 (centre left, top right), 8 (bottom left), 10 (centre bottom, bottom right), 14 (top right), 16 (top centre), 18 (centre top)

Shirley, Clifford: 10 (top left, centre top), 12 (centre left)

Skjold: 3 (bottom left), 11 (centre left), 12 (bottom left), 14 (centre), 20 (centre bottom)

Illustrations

Simon Bull: 19

Carolyn Cox: 1, 12, 13, 14 (top left), 16

Tony De Saulles: title page (centre), 2, 4, 9

Helen Herbert: 6

Rob Howard RIBA: front and back cover

Oxford Illustrators: 17

Contents

1 Welcome!

Have you ever noticed the signs outside church buildings? Think how many of them say, in one way or another, 'Welcome', 'Come in'. Do they mean what they say: to come inside, almost as if it was your home?

Yes, they do. A home is what the church building really is. The word 'church' itself means a group of Christians—people who follow the teaching and example of someone called Jesus Christ. Above all, they believe Jesus has opened the way for them to be members of God's family. The church building is their family home. It's not where they live, but it's where they meet as a family.

▼ **Everyone welcome!**

Everyone is important in God's family, the church. And everyone is welcome to join them—to look, listen, and find out more about their faith in Jesus.

Come in and explore

Christians are very pleased to welcome others. They know that some visitors just come to explore; others come to sit quietly; some want to meet someone who will give them a friendly word—whatever they do or don't believe about Christianity.

This book is designed to help you feel welcome in a church. You'll find out about the buildings and their furniture; you'll also discover what it might be like to come to a church as a special visitor to a family home.

Opening times

Many church buildings are open for visitors to wander into every day. Others are only open when there is a church member there to welcome people.

Did you know?

The first Christians had no special buildings of their own. They would often meet in each other's homes. In fact, in was only when the Roman emperor Constantine became a Christian some 300 years later and made Christianity the official religion of the Roman Empire that it was possible for people to have special buildings.

Jesus Christ and the beginnings of Christianity

The 'Jesus Christ' whom Christians follow is a real person. He was born about 2000 years ago in a province of the Roman Empire—the area that is known today as Israel. Stories say that angels announced his birth and said that he was the Son of God.

Jesus was born a Jew. Like all Jewish boys, he learned about God from the special books of the Jewish faith. These writings included stories about how God made the world and loved it, and how people turned away from God. They also contained promises that God would one day send a special king who would bring people back to God.

When he grew up, Jesus left his work as a builder-carpenter to spend time teaching people about God. He told stories to help them understand that God is kind and loving and wants people to be like that too. He himself made friends with people who were friendless and healed many who were sick. He spoke of a new life for anyone who believed in him. Many people came to believe that he was the promised king—the 'Messiah' or 'Christ'.

However, other people turned against Jesus and arranged to have him put to death using the method of execution the Romans had for common criminals: he was nailed to a cross of wood—crucified.

A few days later Jesus' friends reported that they had seen him alive again. Soon, they were out and about telling people everywhere about Jesus: about the new life God had given him and about God's promise of new life for everyone who followed him. Even their enemies noticed that Christians lived changed lives, loving and helping one another. The message spread quickly. It is still spreading.

◀ **Church guides**

Some churches have guidebooks to tell you about the building.

2 Branches of the same family

Christians believe they are members of the same family. However, over the centuries, different 'branches' of that family developed. Each has its own special traditions.

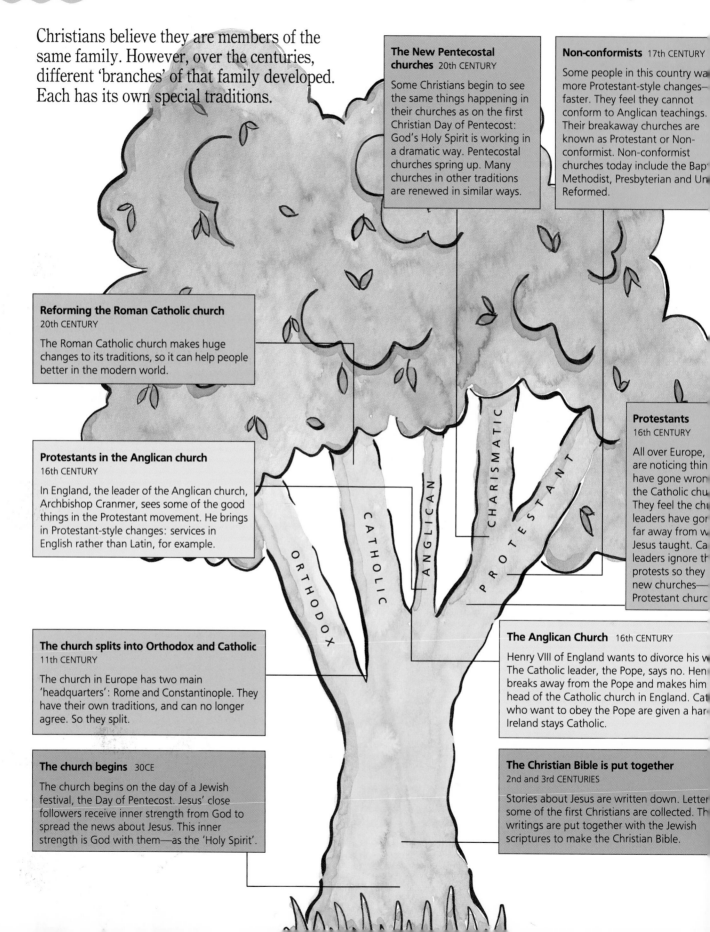

The New Pentecostal churches 20th CENTURY

Some Christians begin to see the same things happening in their churches as on the first Christian Day of Pentecost: God's Holy Spirit is working in a dramatic way. Pentecostal churches spring up. Many churches in other traditions are renewed in similar ways.

Non-conformists 17th CENTURY

Some people in this country wa[nt] more Protestant-style changes— faster. They feel they cannot conform to Anglican teachings. Their breakaway churches are known as Protestant or Non-conformist. Non-conformist churches today include the Bap[tist,] Methodist, Presbyterian and Un[ited] Reformed.

Reforming the Roman Catholic church
20th CENTURY

The Roman Catholic church makes huge changes to its traditions, so it can help people better in the modern world.

Protestants in the Anglican church
16th CENTURY

In England, the leader of the Anglican church, Archbishop Cranmer, sees some of the good things in the Protestant movement. He brings in Protestant-style changes: services in English rather than Latin, for example.

Protestants
16th CENTURY

All over Europe, [people] are noticing thin[gs] have gone wron[g in] the Catholic chu[rch.] They feel the ch[urch] leaders have go[ne] far away from w[hat] Jesus taught. Ca[tholic] leaders ignore th[e] protests so they [set up] new churches— Protestant chur[ches.]

ORTHODOX

CATHOLIC

ANGLICAN

CHARISMATIC

PROTESTANT

The church splits into Orthodox and Catholic
11th CENTURY

The church in Europe has two main 'headquarters': Rome and Constantinople. They have their own traditions, and can no longer agree. So they split.

The Anglican Church 16th CENTURY

Henry VIII of England wants to divorce his w[ife.] The Catholic leader, the Pope, says no. Hen[ry] breaks away from the Pope and makes him[self] head of the Catholic church in England. Ca[tholics] who want to obey the Pope are given a har[d time.] Ireland stays Catholic.

The church begins 30CE

The church begins on the day of a Jewish festival, the Day of Pentecost. Jesus' close followers receive inner strength from God to spread the news about Jesus. This inner strength is God with them—as the 'Holy Spirit'.

The Christian Bible is put together
2nd and 3rd CENTURIES

Stories about Jesus are written down. Letter[s] some of the first Christians are collected. Th[ese] writings are put together with the Jewish scriptures to make the Christian Bible.

Orthodox

In Britain, most Orthodox churches have been set up by people from Eastern Europe. They have not been able to afford the splendid buildings of their homelands—but inside, the church building is often richly decorated.

◀ Icons

Icons are special pictures and an important part of worship in the Orthodox churches. The size of the figures, the way they hold their hands, the way they are dressed and so on all have special meanings that remind people of what they believe.

Anglican (or Episcopalian)

▶ A parish church

Henry VIII took over the Catholic church in this country. But the way the church was organized stayed the same. The country was divided into parishes led by a priest.

Did you know?

The Anglican church is 'established' by law. This law says that its leaders must offer Christian support and help to anyone in their area who asks for it.

▶ The cathedral and the diocese

Parishes are organized into larger groups, each called a diocese. A diocese is led by a bishop from a central town. ('Episcopalian' means 'led by a bishop'.) The central church building is the cathedral.

Non-conformist
▶ A chapel

Protestants thought the Catholic church gave too much attention to having a splendid building. They preferred a plain building, which would not distract people from listening to the Bible and talks explaining what it meant.

Pentecostal

From the outside, Pentecostal churches are much the same as any Non-conformist or Protestant church.

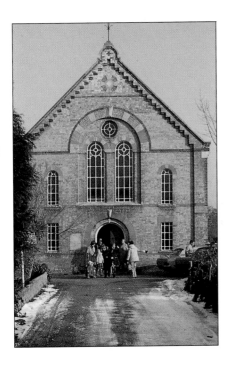

Roman Catholic

Roman Catholics have only been allowed to worship freely in this country in the last 150 years. As their ancient buildings had long been used by the Anglicans, many of their present buildings are quite new.

3 A place to meet with God

Church buildings are places where Christians can meet as God's family. Part of that means meeting with each other. The other part means meeting with God.

All Christians would agree that God is everywhere in the world, and that they can talk to God in prayer at any time and know God is with them anywhere.

Even so, they design their church buildings to be places that will help people think about God and what God is like. There are many different ways of describing God, and many styles of building!

▶ A grand church

This massive church building with its spectacular ornaments and colourful services is like a grand palace. The Christians who built it want to give the message that God is a great ruler—the ruler of the world.

▼ A homely church

This church is plain and comfortable. Christians believe that God came to this world as a human child—that God wants to meet people as they are and make friends with them. Some Christians like their church buildings to feel homely and welcoming.

Can you wander anywhere?

If a church is left open for visitors you are usually welcome to explore everywhere, treating it as carefully as you would want visitors to treat your home. However, some churches have a 'sanctuary', where the service called Holy Communion takes place (see page 13). It is an important part of worshipping God, and members usually stay out of the sanctuary except for the service. Visitors often stay out too.

▼ **A sanctuary**

In a typical sanctuary you will commonly see:

● a table, often called an 'altar'.

● candlesticks, which are lit during services. As a candle helps people find their way in the dark, so

Christians believe Jesus guides them through life.

● a Bible, the special book of the Christian faith.

The bread and wine used during the communion service are laid out here.

◄ **In the round**

Some church buildings have seats arranged in circular fashion around the place where the leaders of the service stand. This arrangement is more like a 'family circle' with God at the centre of the family.

4 A place for God's family

A large part of any church building is designed as a place where people can gather. Christians meet for services in which they can worship God together, and encourage one another.

Did you know?

The people who gather for a church service are called the congregation.

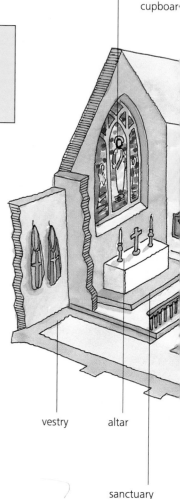

east window

aumbry cupboar

vestry   altar

sanctuary

cho
stal

▲ Please be seated

Church services be anything from half an hour to two hours long. Nowadays most churches have seats for all who come.

In the past, people stood up for the services, and this is still the case in a few churches. However, in the last couple of hundred years most churches have had pews—rows of fixed wooden seats. Pews are useful because they stay put and seat a lot of people. But they're not very comfortable!

In churches where people kneel to pray, the pews may have a built-in 'kneeler'.

◀ Chairs

Movable seats allow people to arrange the room in lots more ways. Many new churches have chosen movable seats, and a number of older ones are replacing some or all of their pews with chairs.

People might arrange these in different ways for different events: a small, mid-week meeting might need just a ring of chairs in a corner somewhere; in some services, Christians might gather in small groups for part of the service, and would move their chairs into groups.

Parts of a church

A traditional parch church may look like this.

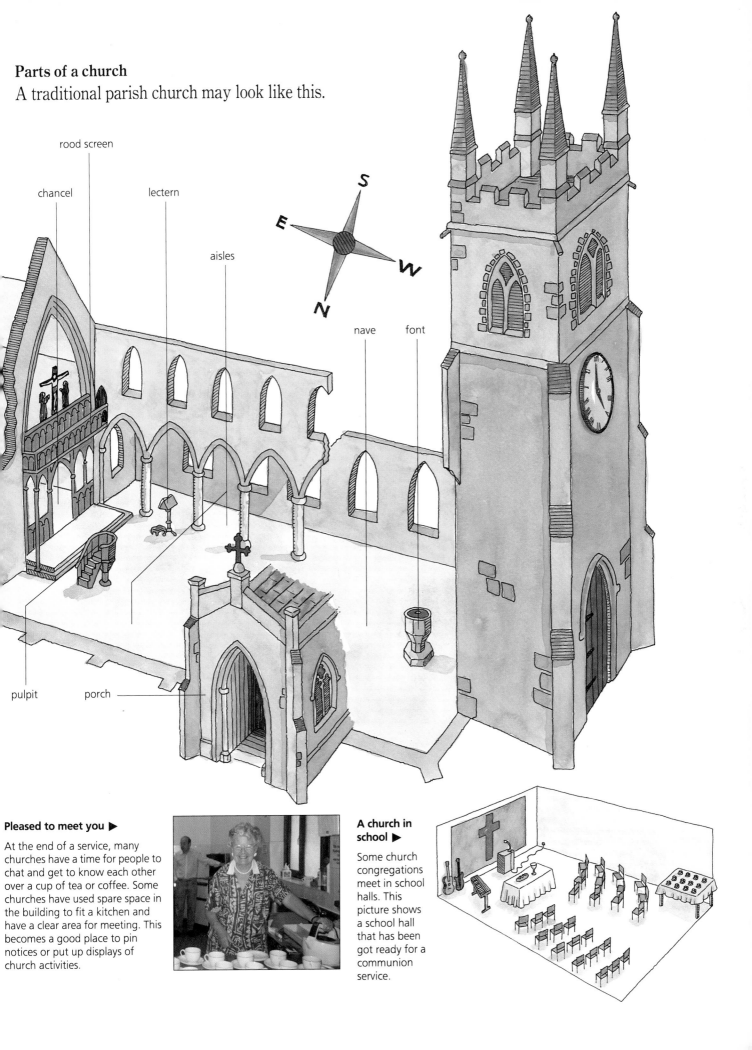

rood screen

chancel

lectern

aisles

S

E

W

N

nave

font

pulpit

porch

Pleased to meet you ▶

At the end of a service, many churches have a time for people to chat and get to know each other over a cup of tea or coffee. Some churches have used spare space in the building to fit a kitchen and have a clear area for meeting. This becomes a good place to pin notices or put up displays of church activities.

A church in school ▶

Some church congregations meet in school halls. This picture shows a school hall that has been got ready for a communion service.

5 Special symbols

In a church, you will see many special designs called symbols. A symbol is much more than a picture of something. It is more like a code or a clue, with a special message for those who understand it.

One symbol you will see in any church is a cross. It might be very large and made of wood, stone or metal; it might be a small ornament; it might be stitched into cloth, or printed on the cover of the service books. You might see all of these types of cross in one church.

The cross is the most important symbol of the Christian church.

◀ The cross

The cross is at the centre of the Christian faith. It reminds Christians of Jesus, of his death on a cross, of the fact that even as he hung dying he forgave his enemies, and shows how God wants to forgive all those who do wrong.

▲ The empty cross

The empty cross reminds them of his coming to life again, and the new life he promises to anyone who believes in him.

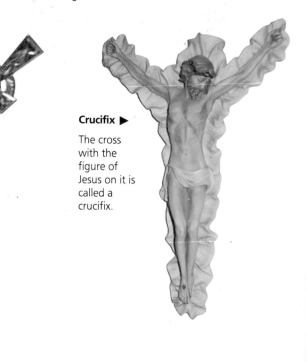

Crucifix ▶

The cross with the figure of Jesus on it is called a crucifix.

◀ The rood and the rood screen

'Rood' is an old word for cross. Many of the parish churches in this country have something called a 'rood screen'. It is, quite simply a screen dividing the people's part of the church from the chancel, the place where the choir sit, and the special 'sanctuary' beyond. On the screen is the 'rood' or cross—usually a carving of Jesus on the cross. The carving often shows two other people. One is Mary, Jesus' mother. The other is John, one of Jesus' closest friends. In the book he wrote about Jesus, John recalls that Jesus asked him to take care of his mother.

Christians walk through the doorway in the screen and approach the sanctuary when they come to take the bread and wine at a communion service. As they walk under the cross, it reminds them that people can only come near to God because Jesus, by his death on a cross, provided a way for anyone to receive God's forgiveness and so belong to God's family.

▼ The Alpha and Omega

Alpha and Omega are the first and last letters of the Greek alphabet, and you may see them written as two letters or combined into a single symbol. The book of Revelation in the Bible includes a dramatic description of the new kingdom that Jesus will establish, which says that he is 'the Alpha and Omega', the first and the last. This symbol reminds Christians that Jesus is the great king for all time.

▼ The Chi-Rho

Chi and Rho are the two Greek letters that begin the Greek word 'Christ'. The Chi-Rho is a symbol that puts the two together. It reminds Christians that Jesus is the 'Christ', or the Messiah: the king whom God promised to send to rescue people.

◀ IHS

The letters IHS are the first three letters of the Greek word for Jesus. However, in the Middle Ages, even church leaders knew more Latin than Greek and they gave the letters other meanings based on Latin words. One of these is Iesus Hominum Salvator—the Latin for 'Jesus, Humankind's Saviour'.

Fish

The fish is secret sign from the early days of Christianity, when it was breaking the law for Christians to meet together. At that time many spoke Greek. The Greek word for fish (ichthus) supplies the first letters for the phrase Jesus Christ, God's Son, Saviour.

Dove ▶

The dove is the sign of the Holy Spirit. The story of Jesus' baptism in the Bible says that as he came up out of the water, the Holy Spirit came down on him in the form of a dove.

6 Important people

The church building you visit may be empty. But a glance around will show that it's taken a lot of work by a lot a people to make it look the way it does. The people who regularly meet there are more important than their building.

◄ A place for everyone

Everyone has a part to play in the church family. Everyone is important—boys and girls, men and women alike.

Who is the most important?

On one occasion, some of Jesus' closest followers were arguing about which of them was the most important.

Jesus called a child and said, 'I assure you that unless you change and become like children, you will never enter the kingdom of heaven. The greatest in the kingdom of heaven is the one who is humble and becomes like this child. And whoever welcomes in my name one such child as this, welcomes me.'

Did you know?

Many churches have full-time leaders, and they are usually in charge of organizing the services. In some churches, they also do the main teaching.

The Orthodox leader is a priest.

The Roman Catholic leader is also called a priest.

In the Anglican church the priest is called a vicar or rector. The assistant is called a deacon or curate.

Protestant and Pentecostal churches use many different names, depending on the type of church. Titles you will hear often are minister and pastor.

► Two leaders

Here a very important leader in the Catholic church – a cardinal – greets the Church of Ireland Archbishop. The Bible teaches that church leaders should help and serve others.

Everyone takes part! To get just one service ready these people . . .

| swept the floor | fixed the dodgy light bulb | arranged the flowers | polished the brass | played the music | acted a |

Special clothes

In some churches the leaders may wear special clothes when they take part in the services. The garments have a symbolic meaning in themselves, and are often decorated with Christian symbols as well.

A large number of the full-time leaders in the church wear a white collar—properly called a clerical collar but nearly always called a dog collar.

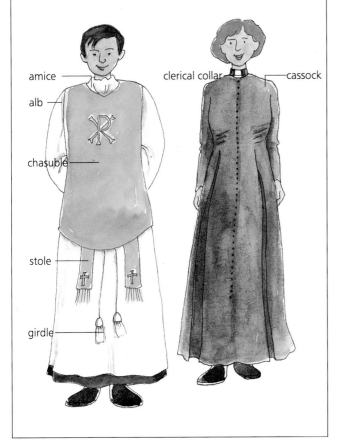

amice
alb
chasuble
stole
girdle

clerical collar — cassock

Important church people in action outside the service . . .

visited someone in hospital

spent time with someone who felt lonely

cooked a splendid meal and invited people to come and share it

made someone a special card to cheer them up

made someone smile

Did you know?

Several branches of the church organize the way they select, train and approve who can be a full-time leader. These selected leaders are often referred to as 'clergy' and the rest of the church as the 'lay people' or 'laity'.

more actors

led the prayers people said aloud

said the prayers and distributed the bread and wine at the service of Holy Communion

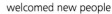
led the singing

welcomed new people

Coming to a service

It can be very interesting to explore an empty church, but it can be hard to guess what some of the furnishings are for. If you could see the church in use, you could work out at least some of the answers right away.

A time to meet

Outside church building you will often see notices inviting anyone to come along and join the Christians who meet there. These notices usually list the times of regular meetings, which are called services. These services have different

The church service: what you need to know

What to wear

Come as you are! If you have a choice, dress as for a family get-together.

What to bring

Nothing needed. There may be a collection—for a charity or for church expenses—so you can bring money for that if you wish.

At the door

Expect a welcome—and the books you'll need for the service. It can be quite a few!

Where to sit

Choose from any of the seats in the main part of the building. One or two may be reserved for someone who has a special job to do in the service. It will be labelled. Don't get stuck behind a pillar!

Will anyone talk to me?

In some churches they might—the whole place might be buzzing with conversation. In others, it might be more usual to spend the minutes before the start quietly, so that those who want to can talk to God in silent prayer. They might bow their heads or kneel as they do so.

names, which may give some idea of what kind of meeting it is going to be—a family service, for example, or evening prayer.

In most churches, a lot of the meetings are held on a Sunday. Christians believe that God wants people to enjoy one day of rest in seven, and this is the special day of the week they have set aside—to rest, and to worship God.

For Christians, Sunday is also a special 'anniversary'. Stories about Jesus Christ say that he was put to death by his enemies on a Friday, but that God raised him to life on a Sunday.

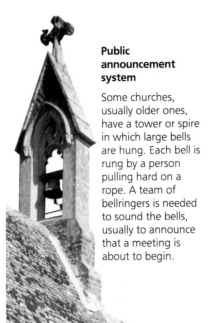

Public announcement system

Some churches, usually older ones, have a tower or spire in which large bells are hung. Each bell is rung by a person pulling hard on a rope. A team of bellringers is needed to sound the bells, usually to announce that a meeting is about to begin.

Beginning

A service may begin with an announcement, a procession, or everyone standing to sing.

Joining in

Throughout the service you're welcome to follow what goes on or simply sit and watch. For example, some Christians raise their arms when singing. You don't have to!

In some services, there may be a moment when the leader invites people to greet one another with 'a sign of peace'. People shake one another by the hand. They might say 'The peace of the Lord be always with you', to which the response is 'And also with you'.

If there's communion

The only time when it matters about being a member is if you go to a service that includes 'communion'—a special event in which Christians share bread and wine (see page 13). This 'meal' is something Jesus told his followers to do, and in many churches the usual practice is to offer this only to people who have joined that church. In others, anyone who is a Christian may receive bread and wine.

Other people are welcome to stay and watch.

Ending

Many church services end with a prayer asking God to help people in their Christian life in the days ahead. There may be a procession out. After a respectful pause, people begin to shuffle and whisper!

And after ...

Most people gather up the things they were handed at the door and take them back. What happens then varies. You'll almost certainly get a handshake from one or more of the people who led the service, and if you want to you can introduce yourself. In some churches you'll have a very warm welcome: people will come to introduce themselves, to find out who you are, to bring you refreshments ...

Singing for God

Whenever you visit a church building, you're likely to find some kind of musical instrument. Music and singing are an important part of many church services. A lot of the songs have words that praise God, to help Christians celebrate together the things they believe God has done for them. Others are songs asking God to help and guide people.

Words, words, words

Many churches have one main hymnbook. They may also have booklets of more recent songs. If the people want to sing a song that is not in one of these books, the words will be printed out on a leaflet or perhaps shown on an overhead projecter. Occasionally, the congregation will sing from memory.

In some services, people may sing in a language and with music you have never heard before. This 'singing in tongues' is something that Christians believe is a special gift from God.

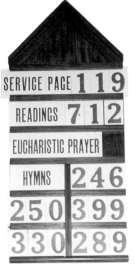

◀ Hymn numbers

You will often see a small board with a list of numbers on it in a church. These are the numbers of the hymns and songs that people will find in their hymnbooks.

◀ Pipe organ

A pipe organ is the musical instrument you will see most often in churches today, and it will be used to lead the singing of the more traditional songs, often with the help of a choir. Pipe organs only became popular for church music from the 1830s onwards. That means they had to be installed—at great upheaval and expense—after the building was in place.

Smaller churches may have a piano, harmonium, or electronic keyboard.

◀ All kinds of music

Different types of Christian songs work best with different types of musical instruments. Church music today is often accompanied by piano, guitar, or small bands or orchestras. This is not new: before the organ became the most common instrument in churches local bands accompanied hymns on instruments such as the flute, bassoon and violin.

◀ Choir

Many churches have choirs: good singers who put in a lot of time practising. However, their music is not meant to be a performance: it is meant to help all Christians worship God through singing.

These choristers are from the choir school at Salisbury Cathedral.

Did you know?

Singing for God dates back to the beginnings of Christianity. Here is a line from a letter written to one of the very first groups of Christians:

'Sing psalms, hymns and sacred songs; sing to God with thanksgiving in your hearts.'

The 'psalms' are the songs found in the special writings of the Jews. The book of Psalms is included in both the Jewish scriptures and the Christians Bible.

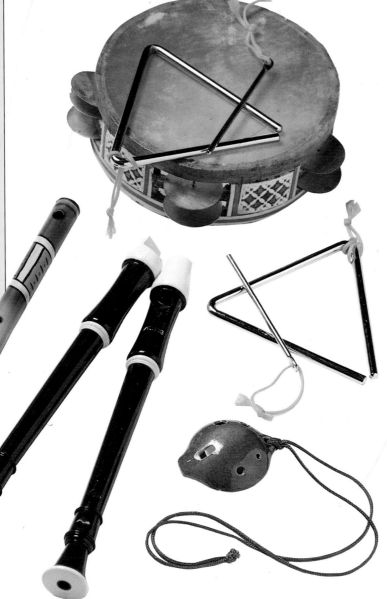

How to sing hymns

John and Charles Wesley were two enthusiastic Christians who lived in the eighteenth century. John Wesley's preaching had great appeal among ordinary people, thousands of whom also became enthusiastic Christians. Charles Wesley wrote many hymns for their services, and a number of these are still hugely popular today.

Here are John Wesley's instructions for how hymns should be sung, written in 1761:

I. Learn these Tunes before you learn any others ...

II. Sing them exactly as they are printed here without altering or mending them at all ...

III. Sing All. See that you join with the congregation as frequently as you can ...

IV: Sing lustily and with a good courage. Beware of singing as if you were half dead, or half asleep; but lift up your voice with strength ...

V: Sing modestly. Do not bawl, so as to be heard above or distinct from the rest of the congregation, that you may not destroy the harmony ...

VI: Sing in Time. Whatever time is sung, be sure to keep with it. Do not run before nor stay behind it ... and take care not to sing too slow ...

VII: Above all sing spiritually. Have an eye to God in every word you sing. Aim at pleasing Him more than yourself or any other creature ...

Learning about God: A special book

When Christians meet as a church, they want to learn about God together. One very important way of doing this is to hear the Bible read aloud. A service will often include two or three readings from the Bible.

◀ Lectern

Most churches have a special stand for their Bible. It is called a lectern, and it holds the book open at a convenient angle for reading.

◀ Introducing the reading

When people read from the Bible in church, they usually give a reference so people can find the passage for themselves—either in a Bible or in the service book. The reference has three main parts:

● the name of the book

● the number of the chapter in that book

● the number of the verse within the chapter

So they might say . . .

The Old Testament lesson is from the book of Genesis, chapter 45, verses 1 to 15.

The New Testament reading is from the Epistle to the Romans, chapter 12 verses 1 to 8.

The Gospel reading is from Mark, chapter 4, starting at verse 3.

Dividing the Bible into chapters and verses is something that was done long after the books were written. The same system is used in Bible translations all over the world.

▼ Bringing the Bible to life

Christians think the actual words in the Bible are very important, and they take time to study them carefully. However, there are many other ways to make the stories 'come alive' for people. In church buildings you will see Bible stories told in many different ways.

Here is a retelling of the story of the sower in stained glass. You can read the words on the Bible page shown on the far left.

MARK 4   49

e Apostles
(2–16)

ill and called
d. They came
ve, whom he
osen you to
"I will also
and you will
emons."
e he chose:
name Peter);
hn, the sons
m the name
Men of Thun-
Bartholomew,
es son of
n the Patriot,
trayed Jesus.

ul
–23; 12.10)
. Again such
at Jesus and
eat. 21 When
they set out
cause people
!"
aw who had
saying, "He
the chief of
the power to

to him and
: "How can
If a country
ich fight each
apart. 25 If a
roups which
will fall apart.
divides into
vill fall apart

nto a strong
is belongings
strong man;
e.
eople can be
all the evil
whoever says
y Spirit will
use he has
30 Jesus said

Jesus' Mother and Brothers
(Matt. 12.46–50; Luke 8.19–21)

31 Then Jesus' mother and brothers arrived. They stood outside the house and sent in a message, asking for him. 32 A crowd was sitting round Jesus, and they said to him, "Look, your mother and your brothers and sisters are outside, and they want you."
33 Jesus answered, "Who is my mother? Who are my brothers?" 34 He looked at the people sitting round him and said, "Look! Here are my mother and my brothers! 35 Whoever does what God wants him to do is my brother, my sister, my mother."

The Parable of the Sower
(Matt. 13.1–9; Luke 8.4–8)

4 Again Jesus began to teach beside Lake Galilee. The crowd that gathered round him was so large that he got into a boat and sat in it. The boat was out in the water, and the crowd stood on the shore at the water's edge. 2 He used parables to teach them many things, saying to them:
3 "Listen! Once there was a man who went out to sow corn. 4 As he scattered the seed in the field, some of it fell along the path, and the birds came and ate it up. 5 Some of it fell on rocky ground, where there was little soil. The seeds soon sprouted, because the soil wasn't deep. 6 Then, when the sun came up, it burnt the young plants; and because the roots had not grown deep enough, the plants soon dried up. 7 Some of the seed fell among thorn bushes, which grew up and choked the plants, and they didn't produce any corn. 8 But some seeds fell in good soil, and the plants sprouted, grew, and produced corn: some had thirty grains, others sixty, and others a hundred."
9 And Jesus concluded, "Listen, then, if you have ears!"

The Purpose of the Parables
(Matt. 13.10–17; Luke 8.9–10)

10 When Jesus was alone, some of those who had heard him came to him with the twelve disciples and asked him to explain the parables. 11 "You have been given the secret of the Kingdom of God," Jesus answered. "But the others, who are

▲ **The Ten commandments**
The Ten commandments are a list of God's standards from some of the oldest books of the Bible. Important Bible passages may be displayed as texts on the walls of churches.

▲ **A children's Bible**
Some of the best-loved stories from the Bible may be retold for young readers in simpler words with bright pictures. This kind of Bible might be used in a church childrens' group.

What is the Bible?

The Bible is the name given to the special book of the Christian faith. Christians believe that the many people who wrote the different books in the Bible were all inspired by God.

The Christian Bible is a collection of books. It can be divided into two sections:

Old Testament—first written in Hebrew

The Law
The earliest books, with stories of the beginning of the nation of Israel—the Jews—and the laws God gave them.

History and Story
These books tell of about 1500 years in the history of the Jewish people from the time they settled the land of Canaan (around 1000 BCE).

Poetry and Wisdom
These books include songs and poems to God and advice on how to live.

Prophets
Warnings and promises from 'prophets'—people who acted as God's messengers to the people.

Deuterocanonical
Additional books including stories and history. These are included in some Bibles.

Did you know?
About three-quarters of the Bible is Old Testament, and a quarter is New Testament. Try opening a Bible three-quarters of the way through, and you'll nearly always open it in one of the first four books of the New Testament: the Gospels of Matthew, Mark, Luke or John.

New Testament—written in Greek

Gospels and Acts
The Gospels are the stories of Jesus' life. The book of Acts is the second part of Luke's gospel, and tells of some of the first Christians.

Letters
Letters from leading Christians to some of the new churches.

A vision
A book told in dramatic picture-language, written to give Christians hope for the future, however much they had to suffer for their faith. It points to a time when Jesus will return and establish a new kingdom.

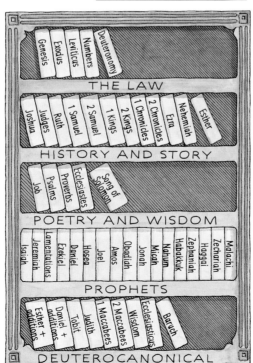

Genesis, Exodus, Leviticus, Numbers, Deuteronomy
THE LAW

Joshua, Judges, Ruth, 1 Samuel, 2 Samuel, 1 Kings, 2 Kings, 1 Chronicles, 2 Chronicles, Ezra, Nehemiah, Esther
HISTORY AND STORY

Job, Psalms, Proverbs, Ecclesiastes, Song of Solomon
POETRY AND WISDOM

Isaiah, Jeremiah, Lamentations, Ezekiel, Daniel, Hosea, Joel, Amos, Obadiah, Jonah, Micah, Nahum, Habakkuk, Zephaniah, Haggai, Zechariah, Malachi
PROPHETS

Esther + additions, Daniel + additions, Tobit, Judith, 1 Maccabees, 2 Maccabees, Wisdom, Ecclesiasticus, Baruch
DEUTEROCANONICAL

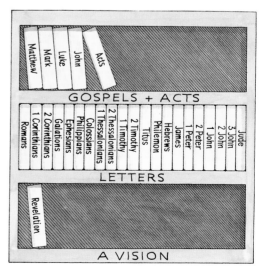

Matthew, Mark, Luke, John, Acts
GOSPELS + ACTS

Romans, 1 Corinthians, 2 Corinthians, Galatians, Ephesians, Philippians, Colossians, 1 Thessalonians, 2 Thessalonians, 1 Timothy, 2 Timothy, Titus, Philemon, Hebrews, James, 1 Peter, 2 Peter, 1 John, 2 John, 3 John, Jude
LETTERS

Revelation
A VISION

Christians meet together to learn more about their faith. In a church service people will spend some time doing just that.

Often they listen to teaching. It may be a talk, called a sermon. A special place is provided where the person giving the talk can stand: the pulpit.

◀ Central pulpit

Some churches have been designed with a high pulpit right at the centre front. The people who built this style of church felt that the teaching was the most important part of the service, so they gave it the most important place in the building.

▼ Side pulpit

This pulpit is to one side of the church, so everyone in the congregation still has a clear view to the 'altar'. When the church was built this was felt to be the most important part of the church.

▼ Learning from one another

Christians believe that everyone is of equal value in God's family, and that they have a lot to learn from each other—not just people who are good at teaching. This kind of learning together often takes place in small discussion groups. Churches that have movable seats can arrange for people to meet in groups for this purpose. In churches with fixed pews, discussion groups often have to take place elsewhere—perhaps in a hall, or in people's homes.

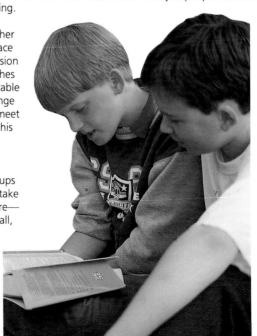

▲ Learning without words

A talk is not the only way to communicate a message. Dance or drama may be used. Some modern churches have planned for these events and have staging. In older churches, people have to make the best use they can of the space available.

Starting young ▶

Christians know that it is important to go on learning about their faith all through life.

A lot of churches provide special opportunities for the children who come to learn about God, Jesus, the Bible, and the church. This may mean having a learning session in a different room at the same time as the main service. It is sometimes called 'Sunday School', but it's usually more like a holiday club than a class.

Gifts of the spirit

Spreading the message ▶

In some places you will see ancient 'preaching crosses' close to churches: the preacher would be outside the building, so that even people walking by might be drawn to listen.

▲ Learning from children

This banner was made by children. The words on it describe the kind of life enjoyed by people who put God first in their lives. It is something everyone can learn from.

◀ Learning about Jesus

A model of one of the 'wise men' who came to visit the baby Jesus.

Did you know?

From the very beginning, Christians have been keen to spread the news about Jesus wherever they can. The Bible tells us that soon after Jesus had returned to heaven, his close follower Peter preached to the crowds thronging the streets in Jerusalem. About three thousand people became Christians that same day, and asked to be baptized.

◀ Teaching out of doors

Nowadays, you may find Christians spreading the message of their faith in shopping precincts, at fairs, on beaches . . . wherever there are people who might be interested.

11 Talking to God

Christians believe that they can talk to God anywhere and any time. They can listen to God too: answers come in different ways, such as 'loud thoughts' that won't go away, or as words from the Bible that suddenly seem very special. When they meet as a church, they will talk and listen to God together: they will pray.

Many people find that a quiet church building provides a place where it is easier for them to pray than anywhere else.

During a service, there are usually several times of prayer that is spoken aloud. Some churches have 'set' prayers that can be read. In others, Christians simply speak to God as they would speak to anyone. Sometimes there is one person leading the prayers. Or there may be a time of 'open' prayer, when anyone who wishes to is invited to say a prayer aloud.

The Lord's Prayer

Jesus' first followers on this earth noticed that he spent a lot of time talking to God in prayer, and they asked him to teach them to pray. The prayer he gave them is said aloud in most churches. It is sometimes called the Lord's Prayer, sometimes the 'Our Father', and sometimes the Latin for 'Our Father': 'Paternoster'.

Our Father in heaven,
hallowed be your name,
your kingdom come,
your will be done,
on earth as in heaven.
Give us today our daily bread.
Forgive us sins
as we forgive those who sin
  against us.
Lead us not into temptation
but deliver us from evil.

This traditional ending has been added by Christians since very early times:

For the kingdom, the power,
and the glory are yours
now and for ever. Amen.

Kneeling

In some churches, it is the custom for people to kneel to pray. Kneeling on a wooden or stone floor is uncomfortable, so padded kneelers are usually provided. Sometimes these are worked in needlepoint, with colourful designs and pictures. These might be based on Bible stories, or symbols of Christianity or the local church, or even of things that are valued in the local community, such as wild flowers and animals.

In other churches, people simply sit to pray. In Roman Catholic and Orthodox churches it is usual to stand up.

A rosary

Some Christians find it helpful to use a string of beads called a rosary when they pray. Each 'bead' reminds them of a prayer to say. The 'set' prayers are called the Our Father, the Hail Mary and the Glory Be—in each case these are the first words of the prayer!

Prayers for all reasons

Christians pray for all kinds of reasons: to say thank you to God, to say sorry, to ask God for things. In many church services these prayers are said:

● A collect

In some churches there is a special set prayer for each day. This is called the collect.

● Prayers of praise and thanksgiving ▶

Christians thank God for all the good things they enjoy—God's world, the delight of being part of God's family, knowing that God is with them always.

● Prayers of confession ▶

Christians believe that God wants to forgive them the wrong they have done and help them live in a good way. Many services provide an opportunity for them to say sorry for their mistakes.

Friends with God

Some christians encourage their members to confess to the priest the wrong they have done, in a private room in the church. The priest advises them on how to put things rights. Catholics call this process is called the 'Sacrament of reconciliation'. 'Reconciliation' means becoming friends again—friends with God.

Candles

In some churches there is a place where anyone can buy a candle and leave it burning. As the person lights it, they will say a prayer—perhaps for some special need they have. The little point of light in a rather dark building is like a picture of the hope they have—that God will hear their prayer and help them in what can seem a dark and difficult problem.

● Intercesssions ▶

Christians believe that God wants to do good things for them. They tell God about their own needs, the needs of fellow Christians, and of the whole world in prayers of intercession.

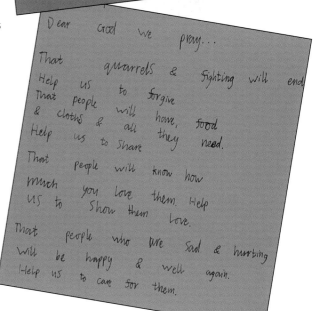

> Dear God
> Thank you for the World you have made. Thank you for the animals that live in this world too. Thank you for plants, flowers and harvest crops. Thank you for giving us friends and families to love us. Thank you that we can call you father, that we are your children.

> Dear God
> you are loving & kind & forgiving to us.
> You want us to be loving to others.
> Sometimes we aren't. We leave people on their own, with no one to talk to. We don't share the good things we have. We tease & bully & hurt. we are sorry. please forgive us please Show us more of your love every day. So we can learn to be more like you.

> Dear God we pray...
> That quarrels & fighting will end Help us to forgive That people will have, food & cloths & all they need. Help us to share.
> That people will know how much you love them. Help us to show them love.
> That people who are sad & hurting will be happy & well again. Help us to care for them.

12 Joining God's family

Anyone is welcome to come into a church as a visitor. Those who decide to follow Jesus become part of God's family, and Christians have a special ceremony to mark the event: baptism. This ceremony involves either dipping the new Christian in water or pouring water over them—usually just over their head.

Some churches baptize people when they are old enough to decide for themselves that they want to be followers of Jesus.

Others baptize infants. Families who want to raise their child as a Christian make promises to give them the teaching and the encouragement they need to learn to be followers of Jesus and then have their child baptized. There is usually some kind of ceremony a few years later when the person baptized can 'confirm' the promises for themselves.

Some churches have special services set aside for baptizing people. Often, however, a baptism is part of the main Sunday service.

A baby is baptized ▶

In the Orthodox and some Catholic churches a baby is dipped right under water for the baptism.

◀ Starting a new life

This baptistry is large enough to allow the baptizer to dip the person being baptized under water for a moment.

One of the ways of understanding what it means to become a Christian is that a person is dying to their old life and being raised to new life as a child of God's family. This style of baptism helps bring out that meaning.

Confirmation

In this confirmation ceremony a young person has made her promise to continue in the Christian life. A bishop is making the sign of the cross on her forehead.

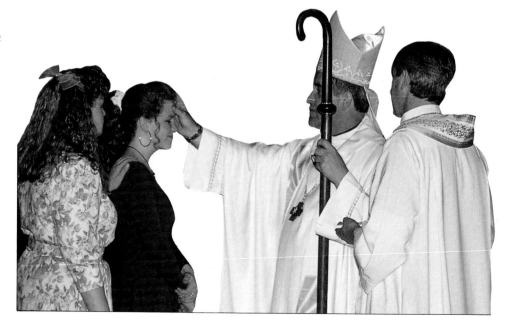

Washed clean ▶

Many churches have a small raised basin called a font. Only a little water need be put in the font to baptize a person by pouring water over their head. This style of baptism helps people think of their becoming a Christian as a washing away of their wrongdoing, and their promise to make a clean, fresh start by living as God wants.

Did you know?

In many older churches, and some newer ones, the font is near one of the doors from which you enter the church building. It helps make the point that a person is baptised when they enter the church family.

▼ Shell scoop

The water may be scooped up from the font in a small silver shell, and then poured over the forehead of the person being baptised.

The person may be given a lighted candle to hold, to remind them that by joining God's family they have passed from darkness to light. In the Anglican service of baptism, the congregation may then say:

Shine as a light in the world to the glory of God the Father.

Jesus' baptism

Jesus was baptized in the River Jordan. The person who baptized him was his own cousin, John, known as John the Baptizer or John the Baptist. It is said that when Jesus was lifted up out of the water, the Holy Spirit in the form of a dove came and settled on him, and a voice from heaven said: 'You are my own dear Son. I am pleased with you.'

This event marked the beginning of Jesus' work of telling people about God.

▼ Baptism gifts

Family and friends often bring gifts when a baby is baptized. It is usual to choose gifts that will help the child learn more of what it means to live as a Christian.

The Lord's Prayer for Children

When a Roman officer named Cornelius heard about Jesus and wanted to follow him, not only was he baptized, but also everyone in his household.

An important official in the Ethiopian court met a Christian named Philip while they were travelling along the same road. The official decided to become a Christian right away. As soon as they came to a place where there was water, he asked to be baptized on the spot.

A special meal

In many church buildings, you will see a large table placed in an important position, usually with the seats facing it. It is called an altar in some churches, and in others a communion table. It is the place where a special meal is shared.

Many names

This meal has different names in different churches: 'Mass', 'the Liturgy', 'Eucharist', 'Holy Communion', 'the Lord's Supper' or simply 'the breaking of bread'.

Wherever it is celebrated, it is the most important ceremony of all for members of God's family, the church. In some churches, such as the Roman Catholic church, there are services of mass every day. Many Anglican churches have holy communion at least once a week. In both cases there are often several services on Sunday, so that everyone who wants to take part can be sure to find a time that suits them.

Other churches celebrate communion less frequently: once a month, perhaps. In some churches people think it is so important that they treat it as a once-a-year event.

There are very few groups of Christians who never hold a special communion service together.

The first special meal—and what it means

On the night when Jesus was betrayed to his enemies, he was sharing a meal with his closest friends. It was the meal to celebrate a Jewish festival called Passover. The Jews remembered how God had rescued them when they were slaves in Egypt. Then, Moses had led them to a new land. On the way, God made an agreement—a covenant—to be their God, and the Jews, to be God's people.

Jesus took the bread that was part of the meal, gave thanks to God, broke it, and said, 'This is my body, which is for you. Eat this and remember me.'

After the supper he took the cup of wine and said, 'This is my blood, the sign of God's new agreement with you. My blood is going to be shed for you. Drink it and remember me.'

The next day, Jesus was put to death. Three days later, God gave him new life.

Christians believe that when they share this meal, they tell about Jesus' death—and also about the good news of God's new agreement: to give new life to all who follow Jesus.

Communion ▶

Christians meet to share a special meal of bread and wine. It is usually laid out on a large table in the church, called an altar or communion table.

◀ Safe keeping

In some churches, more bread and wine than is needed for the congregation is prepared during a service. These elements are then kept safe in a cupboard near the altar–the 'aumbry cupboard' or 'tabernacle'. A light will be kept burning (or switched on!) close by to remind people of their belief that Jesus is really there with them in the communion.

The prepared elements are also used to take to sick people in their homes, so they can have communion too.

Different forms of bread and wine

A silver chalice for the wine and a silver patten for the special wafers used in many Anglican communion services.

The bread and wine shared at communion may look like this. Breaking the one loaf and sharing it reminds Christians that they are one body— people who share in what Jesus offers.

Non-conformist churches usually have a tiny glass of non-alcoholic grape juice and a cube of bread for everyone taking communion.

Christmas is a time for special celebrations in the church. It is the time when Christians remember the birth of Jesus.

▲ **Christmas Day**

Christmas Day is the time when Christians remember the events of Jesus' birth—sometimes called the Nativity. A crib scene may be on display in the church.

The book Luke wrote about Jesus tells the story of a young couple called Mary and Joseph, travelling to Bethlehem to take part in a census organized by the Romans who ruled the land. Mary was pregnant—an angel had told her that her baby was special, God's son. But there was no fine room where this baby could be born: Mary had to take shelter in an animal room and use an animal feed trough, a manger, as her baby's cradle.

Shepherds were out on the hillside nearby, watching their sheep. Angels appeared in the sky, and told them that the one God had promised to send to rescue the world had been born, and was lying in a manger. They came, and found him, just as the angels had said.

Advent: getting ready

Many churches have a yearly pattern of celebrations. It is planned to help people remember events in the life of Jesus. Looking forward to Jesus' birth begins four Sundays before Christmas. This period is called Advent (from a Latin word meaning 'coming') and is a time for getting ready for Jesus' coming. During this time of the church year, Christians often read the passages in the Old Testament that tell of the Jewish people's hope that God would one day send a Messiah, a special king—a 'Christ'.

Advent wreath ▲

The advent wreath is a traditional church decoration. One candle is lit during the service on the first Sunday in Advent. On the second, that candle and another are lit . . .and so on for four Sundays. On Christmas Day, the centre candle is lit. This candle stands for the light and joy Christians believe Jesus has brought into a world that is dark and sad.

Nativity play ▶

In many churches the story of Jesus' birth will be retold in a 'Nativity play'. Nativity means birth.

◄ Epiphany

Twelve days after Christmas many churches will add more figures to the crib scene. The book Matthew wrote about Jesus describes how people who studied the stars came from other lands to find the king whose star they had seen in the sky. The star led them to the house where Jesus was with his mother, Mary. They brought him rich gifts of gold, frankincense and myrrh.

Because there are three gifts named, many crib scenes put three gift-bringers in their scene, even though Matthew doesn't say how many there were. They are often referred to as 'the three wise men'.

This time of the church year is called Epiphany—a word that means 'showing', because Jesus was shown to people representing the nations of the world.

Christingle

Some churches have Christmas services at which a 'Christingle' is given to each child who comes. Each part of the Christingle has a special meaning:

orange: the world

sweets and nuts: the fruits of the earth

candle: Jesus, the 'light of the world'

red ribbon: Jesus' blood, because Jesus died to show God's love for the world

A symbol of life

Evergreens are often used to help decorate the church at Christmas. Their green colour in cold of winter, when other plants are dead and bare, is a reminder to Christians of the new life that Jesus brings, the life that death can never beat.

Carols

In many churches, Christians sing carols—especially joyful songs. Here is a traditional carol:

Rejoice and be merry in
songs and in mirth!
O praise our Redeemer,
all mortals on earth!
For this is the birthday of Jesus our King,
Who brought us salvation—his praises we'll sing!

A heavenly vision appeared in the sky;
Vast numbers of angels the shepherds did spy,
Proclaiming the birthday of Jesus our King,
Who brought us salvation—his praises we'll sing!

Likewise a bright star in the sky did appear,
Which led the Wise Men from the east to draw near;
They found the Messiah, sweet Jesus our King,
Who brought us salvation—his praises we'll sing!

And they were come, they their treasures unfold,
And unto him offered myrrh, incense and gold.
So blessèd for ever be Jesus our King,
Who brought us salvation—his praises we'll sing.

Here are some important words from the carol:

● Redeemer: someone who buys a slave to set them free

● Salvation: rescue

● Messiah: the Hebrew word for Christ—a person marked out by God to be a king

Christians believe that Jesus is God's king, sent specially to rescue people from the dark power of evil and set them free to live as God wants, as members of God's family.

31st. ED

THE CHURCH OF THE NATIVITY, BETHLEHEM

BETHLEHEM CAROL SHEET

Lent

In the weeks before Easter, many church buildings will look extra plain. There will be no flower arrangements. In some churches, pictures will be covered over. That is because it is a solemn time in the church year: the time of Lent.

Christians remember that after Jesus was baptized, he went out into a desert region for forty days. There he went without food—fasted—and spent time thinking about the work that lay ahead of him. He was tempted to give up even before he had begun, but he put these temptations behind him and set out to do the work of making God and people friends again.

Lent begins forty days before Easter. In some church traditions, Sundays are not counted, so Lent actually begins rather more than forty days before!

Ash Wednesday ▶

The first day of Lent is called Ash Wednesday. Christians in some churches meet for a special service to say sorry to God for the wrong they have done. A traditional part of the service is that the palm crosses handed out on Palm Sunday the year before are burned. The priest dips a thumb in the ash and marks a cross on the foreheads of those taking part in the service as a sign of their being sorry.

◀ Mothering Sunday

Mothering Sunday is a day of celebration in the middle of Lent. In the past, it was a special holiday that gave people the chance to go home to their mother church, and visit their families. Nowadays, it is a day when people say thank you to their mothers. One church tradition is to provide posies of flowers for people to give to their mothers.

▼ Palm Sunday ▶

Palm Sunday is the last Sunday before Easter, and the day when Christians remember how Jesus rode into Jerusalem and was greeted like a king. Enthusiastic crowds waved palm branches—yet within a week, they were to turn against him, and let him be crucified. The events of this week are remembered in what is sometimes called 'Holy Week'.

Today, many churches process around their community waving palms before going into the church building. Crosses woven from palm leaves are given out to wave.

Maundy Thursday ▶

A bowl of water and a towel might seem unlikely things for a service! But you might well see them on Maundy Thursday, in Holy Week. The name comes from a Latin word meaning 'commandment', because on that night, when Jesus shared his last meal with his friends, he said this: 'I am giving you a new commandment: love one another, as I have loved you.'

He showed his love for his friends right then and there, by doing the job that no one else wanted: washing everyone's grubby feet. Only a servant would normally have to do that. He told his followers that they should be willing to wash each others feet. In some churches, there is a service that includes a ceremony of foot washing.

A bare church

After the meal, when Jesus shared the bread and wine of the Passover with his friends, he went out to pray. But one of his friends had slipped away to tell his enemies where they could find him and arrest him. In some churches, the altar and the sanctuary are stripped bare. The empty scene helps people think about the awful aloneness of Jesus on that night—his enemies came to take him and his friends ran away.

▼ Good Friday

On Good Friday, some churches recall the terrible journey Jesus had to make from the place where he was handed over to the Roman soldiers in charge of carrying out executions in Jerusalem to the place where they crucified him. They set up points in the church called 'the stations of the cross', and remember not only what happened, but also how the people who were there must have felt, and how they might have acted.

In some churches, there are pictures or carvings for each station of the cross all year round. In others, they are put up only for this special time of year.

The crown of thorns is something the Roman soldiers crammed on to Jesus' head as part of making fun of him as a failed king.

Easter joy

A church building is at its most festive on Easter Day. It is a time to celebrate the greatest news of all in the Christian faith: Jesus rose from the grave; death was beaten; Jesus offers new life to all who follow him.

The first Easter

The Bible stories about Jesus say that after he died, his friends took the body to put in a tomb. They had to hurry, as the Jewish Sabbath was about to begin—the special day of the week set aside to worship God, when no work should be done. They wrapped the body quickly in linen cloth and laid the body on a ledge in a traditional stone-cut tomb and rolled a disc-shaped door stone into place.

When the Sabbath was over, some of the friends went back to the tomb to complete the burial customs—putting spices on the body and wrapping it in more linen cloth before sealing up the door for a year or more, until the body decomposed. To their amazement, the stone was already rolled away, and the body had gone, although the cloths were still there. According to Luke, two figures in bright shining clothes appeared and said 'Why are you looking among the dead for one who is alive? He is not here. He has been raised.' Later that same day, and again for forty days afterwards, many of Jesus friends saw him. God had given him new life.

This special coming alive is often called the resurrection.

Easter sunrise ▶

Many Easter Day services are not in a church building at all. Christians meet out of doors to wait for the sunrise. At the first sign of light, they sing to celebrate Jesus' victory over all the dark powers of evil.

Did you know?

Easter is known as a 'movable feast'—it is a celebration that doesn't have a fixed date, but one that has to be worked out. Churches that have developed out of the Roman Catholic tradition (Anglican and Protestant churches) work it out like this:

● Find the equinox—the day in spring when day and night are the same length. This is a day towards the end of March.

● When is the next full moon after the equinox? (This varies from year to year.)

● Easter falls on the first Sunday after the full moon.

The Eastern churches have a different way of setting the date.

Easter flowers ▶

In this country, Easter is in springtime when many flowers are a reminder of new life after the deadness of winter. Flowers are used in churches to make beautiful displays. In some places, people buy flowers to help remember loved ones who have died. These are used in the flower arrangements, and help people remember although death has taken their loved ones away, it is not the end.

Eggs ▲

Eggs are a reminder of Jesus' tomb—they look like stone, but there is new life within. Chocolate eggs may be handed out to children in church on Easter Sunday as part of the celebration.

Easter garden ▶

Some churches build a miniature Easter Garden. It includes a hill with three crosses—Jesus was crucified along with two criminals— and a tomb in a rock-cut cave close by. The 'stone' is rolled away. On Easter Day itself, a candle near the tomb may be lit, a reminder of Jesus' new life.

Sometimes little models of the friends who came to the tomb are added. Sometimes a candle is lit for each of them.

Paschal candle ▶

The Easter candle, or Paschal candle, is lit at the midnight service before Easter Day. It is lit at all services for the next forty days— the time when Jesus is said to finally gone to be with God.

Did you know?

Some Easter services start off in total darkness. Then the story of people discovering that Jesus had been raised from the dead is read, a light is struck at the altar. Everyone has been given a candle, and the flame is passed along till everyone has a lit candle, and the building is flooded with light.

A year of celebrations

Christmas and Easter are the church festivals that celebrate the most important events in Jesus life: his birth, and his death and resurrection.

Here is the remainder of the church year.

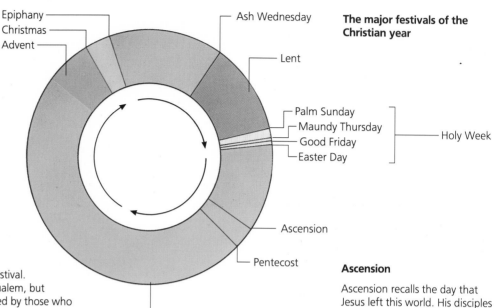

The major festivals of the Christian year

- Epiphany
- Christmas
- Advent
- Ash Wednesday
- Lent
- Palm Sunday
- Maundy Thursday — Holy Week
- Good Friday
- Easter Day
- Ascension
- Pentecost
- Trinity

Pentecost

Pentecost is the name of a Jewish festival. Jesus' closest followers were in Jersualem, but they were still afraid of being arrested by those who had had Jesus killed. It was then that they received the Holy Spirit. They boldly went out to spread the message about Jesus. This day is celebrated as the birthday of the church, because thousands of people believed what Peter had to say about Jesus and became Christians too.

Ascension

Ascension recalls the day that Jesus left this world. His disciples claimed that he was taken up into heaven. Before he went, he promised to send his disciples a 'helper'—the Holy Spirit, who would help them to follow him.

Saints

Some churches set aside a day to remember Christians from long ago who were shining examples of how to follow Jesus. They are called saints.

Some of these are Christians who are named in the New Testament: Matthew, Mark, Luke and John are all saints. So is someone named Paul, who worked hard spreading the message of Jesus and wrote letters to new Christians, some of which are now in the Bible.

Other saints are Christians from later centuries. Some are known all over the world; others, only in their local area.

Churches vary a great deal in whether or not they celebrate saint's days. However, a great many churches are 'dedicated' to a particular saint—and the church may be known by the saint's name—'St Mary's', for example, or 'St Thomas'. It is usual for these churches to remember that saint on their special day.

St Patrick of Ireland ▶
▼ St David of Wales

Both saints worked hard telling people about Jesus.

St PATRICK AT SLEMISH

Colours

Many churches are decked out in hangings of different colours to suit the season of the church year, and the clergy may wear robes of the same colour.

A stole is one of the special items of clothing worn by some church leaders during a service. Different colours are worn for different festivals and seasons of the church year.

Green is worn between Epiphany and Lent, and all through the long season of Trinity

White (here richly decorated with gold and other colours) for Christmas, Easter and Ascension

Violet for Advent and Lent

Red for Palm Sunday, Holy Week, Pentecost

Mary, the Mother of Jesus

In some churches you will see pictures and statues of a woman with a child. This is Mary, the mother of Jesus. All Christians agree that she is unique among the followers of Jesus—being specially chosen to bear God's son.

Some churches celebrate special festivals remembering important events in her life: the day she was conceived, the day an angel told her she would be the mother of Jesus, and the day she went to be with God.

Did you know?

According to the Bible, anyone who believes in Jesus and tries to follow him is a saint.

Chapels

Some churches have smaller 'rooms' to the side of the main part of the church, which are known as chapels.

Often, chapels are set aside to remember a particular saint, and there may be a window, banner or statue of the saint in there.

The aumbry cupboard (see page 13) may well be in the chapel.

Family and community

Christians believe that following Jesus should affect every part of their lives. Important events in the life of each family and of the community are therefore something to share with God.

A funeral

Like everyone, Christians are sad when a family member dies, and they want to remember the person in a good way. Churches often contain memorials to Christians who have died. Some are even buried in the church.

▼ A wedding

Flowers are a traditional way of decorating the church for a wedding. During the wedding, a couple make promises to God to love and support each other for all of their lives. Prayers are said, asking God to help them to keep these important promises.

Graveyard ▶

Many older churches are surrounded by a piece of land that has been used as a graveyard. The graves are often marked by tombstones. These often say who has been buried there and perhaps something about that person's life and family.

Memorial ▶

Some churches contain an effigy —a life-sized carving of a dead person— placed on top of their tomb. This picture shows effigies of three members of the same family arranged on shelves.

▼ A lych gate

The word 'lych' means 'coffin'. Lych gates date from church building traditions of several centuries ago. The coffin would be brought to the church as soon as practical, and it was necessary to provide somewhere where it could rest, sheltered from the weather, until the funeral.

▲ Memorial

This flower pedestal is a memorial. You can see the inscription of the person's name on the base. The flower displays arranged on it each week help the relatives remember their loved one in a cheerful way.

Harvest time ▶

Many churches hold a special service at harvest time when Christians give special thanks to God for giving them the things they need. In rural areas, people may make a special display of farm crops. In others, keen gardeners will bring in some of their harvest.

In places where most of the congregation earn a wage it is more likely they will buy goods from shops and bring those to decorate the church for the thanksgiving service.

After the service the food is usually taken to people in need of it—perhaps to places that provide free meals to the homeless.

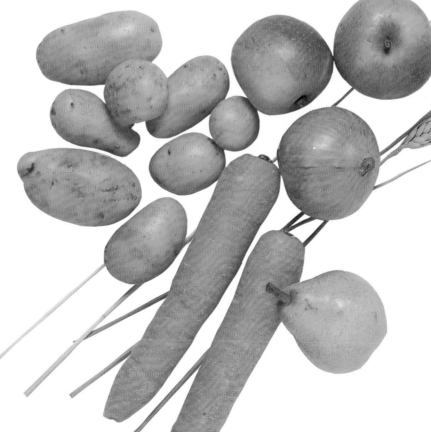

19 A Christian heritage

Many of the things used in churches today date back to long ago. Christians are glad to have this rich heritage.

I believe

What do Christians really believe? In the centuries following the death and resurrection of Jesus, Christians had to think hard about this. After many debates, they came up with statements of belief, each called a 'creed', from the Latin word for 'I believe'. Here is one creed that is said aloud by all the congregation in many churches today— and a fragment of the creed that was painted up in the church years ago.

I believe in God the Father almighty,
Maker of heaven and earth.
I believe in Jesus Christ, God's only Son, our Lord.
He was conceived by the power of the Holy Spirit,
and born of the Virgin Mary.
He suffered under Pontius Pilate,
was crucified, died and was buried.
He descended to the dead.
On the third day he rose again.
He ascended into heaven,
and is seated at the right hand of God the Father.
He will come again to judge the living and the dead.
I believe in the Holy Spirit,
the holy catholic church,
the communion of saints,
the forgiveness of sins,
ther resurrection of the body,
and the life everlasting.

▲ **A shared faith**

The creed is displayed in this church alongside the Ten Commandments and the Lord's Prayer.

Prayers

Just as in ordinary conversation people sometimes like to borrow sayings from other people, so the prayers that other Christians have written can help them in their prayers to God.

Collections of prayers can be found in many churches.

Service books

The Book of Common Prayer has been the starting point for worship in the Church of England since the sixteenth century, when King Henry broke from the Catholic church. It was the work of a leading bishop, Archbishop Cranmer, and helped bring many Protestant changes to the church of his day.

The beautiful old language is rather hard to understand nowadays. In recent years, services with more up-to-date English have been created. The Alternative Service Book contains a wide selection of these.

Church buildings

Throughout the centuries, skilled craftworkers have been delighted to show their enthusiasm for their faith by making beautiful buildings and objects to go in them. The oldest churches in this country date back about a thousand years, and you can often find something added by Christians from every century. They remind Christians today of the faith of Christians from years ago.

▲ Looking at windows ▶

Windows were built in different shapes at different times. By looking at the windows you can often tell when they were built.

from 900 to 1100

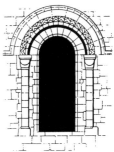

1100 to 1200

1200 to 1300

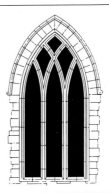

1300 to 1400

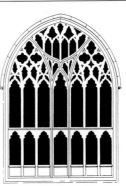

1400 to 1500

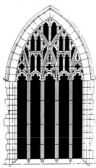
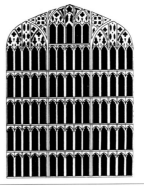

20 Not just a building

Visiting a church can be a real discovery tour. The building itself gives clues about the Christian faith, and the Christians who have worshipped there. The church services that take place can tell you even more.

But a church building isn't just for services!

Parents of small children meet for a mid-week chat.

Many activities

Some of the oldest and most precious church buildings in this country today have seen many different activities within their walls.

Before pews became common, just a couple of hundred years ago, the people's part of the church, the nave, was empty. Few minded standing for the services (there was often a bench built around the wall for those who preferred to sit) and the large, empty area that could be used for lots of other activities during the week. The 'people's' part of the church was used as a community meeting place, much as community halls are used today.

In recent years, many church congregations have done the same. After a service, they clear aside the seating so the space can be used for other activities.

Enter mid-week and you might find all kinds of activities going on: toddlers tumbling around in their playgroup, older people meeting for coffee and chat, people sorting second-hand items to give or sell to people in need ... It all depends on how Christians feel they can best help meet the needs of the community.

A small shop sells Christian books, church guidebooks and souvenirs to weekday visitors.

The work of the church

One church service ends with these words:
'Send us out
in the power of your spirit
to live and work
to your praise and glory. Amen.'

The people not the building

The most important thing to remember is that the church is the people, not the building. To discover a church, you need to discover the Christians, as they seek to follow Jesus and show love to others— the kind of love they believe God shows them.

The church in action
Pictures clockwise from the top:

Young people soon to be confirmed enjoying spending time together.

A sponsored cycle ride from church to church to raise money and get to know people from local churches.

Part of the church family enjoying a summer holiday together.

Young Christians giving a hand with someone else's gardening.

A card made by a young Christian to cheer an elderly church member in hospital.

Index